Ink spilled all over the leaves

Ink spilled all over the leaves

MAHIMA SINGH

PAPER TOWNS
PUBLISHERS

PAPER TOWNS
PUBLISHERS

First published by
Papertowns Publishers
72, Vishwanath Dham Colony,
Niwaru Road, Jhotwara,
Jaipur, 302012

ISBN Print Book - 978-93-91228-09-5

Cover Design by Mahima singh
freakingfreya333@gmail.com

AUTHOR BIO

Mahima Singh Thakur, a 21-year-old computer science student, found herself lost in the world of books in her preteen years as a hand-me-down trait from her Mumma and Nani, and the best one in her opinion. But she didn't stumble upon the magical flawlessness of poetry until the age of sixteen when she came across a second-hand book, a collection of poems by various famous poets, including her forever favourite, Emily Dickinson. At that point, she knew, no matter where life tossed her, she would happily trudge through everything with her love of poetry.

She loves exploring everything mundane in hopes of living her life parallel to a Studio Ghibli character. And while she's not lost in her own world, she works for Nazli, a non-profit organization and as a content writer for Rise Women, a community for changemakers.

Being an introvert, Mahima found writing as a way not to escape, but to help her be more intune with herself and the people in her life. Ink Spilled All Over The Leaves is her first book, and she hopes it lands in the hands of someone who would truly appreciate it.

ACKNOWLEDGEMENT

It's a good feeling to know that I can count on people who exist outside my fictional world of books and films, and I want to thank all of them.

I wrote this book alone, but it only came so far because of you guys!

Arpita, thank you for being you and a kindred spirit.

To the people who make my life more beautiful just by existing: Vaishnavi, Rishika, Dhanu, and Shruti - Thank you for encouraging me throughout this journey.

Thank you,Rinkle, for making me realize how much power and beauty our imaginations can hold.

Thank you, T.S, for being my role model since I was nine years old.

Thank you to everyone who became the Muse of this book at a time when it seemed like all the colours of the world were fading away.

A big thanks to Paper Towns publishers for making my dream come true!

And finally, thank you to my family for everything. I will forever be grateful to each of you.

March

Before march begins,
Let me be kind and carefully honest!
To leave behind magical endlessness.

Let me unravel parts of you,
I might never see them ever again.

Let my fears turn old and grey,
While I appreciate their fine absence.

Let me know how safe feels again,
For 24 hours stay only in my head.

Let us alter ourselves into freaks,
Maybe we will never fall under the graves.

Let us pause the time before its great triumph,
And rebuff its broken fate,
_Before march begins again.

Long-distance

Typically I meet you in the streets,
Now we are in the middle of grief.
For not being,
Like we were before your cab slid in the grid.
I mostly catch you in my dreams,
Now you watch me back through a time-constrained screen,
As if you are preserved in a glass over these pastel sheets.
I knew you more
When I didn't know you
Now I know you very little
That the world has carved_
Some limits.
But I'll know you,
When it's time,
And if not_
Then it's a failure on the time's side.

April

At last, the night is not perched upon my eyes,
And the sun has become my friend again.
But I have made another friend too,
Taller but small enough to let the giant star,
Float around in clouds in its glory.
We talk through my tiny screen, held
Between my cold immersed fingers,
Makes me look like a reckless man,
And an innocent child stitched together.
Like flowers around long cable wires.
They say the early signs of summer look the same,
Which might have offended me a little,
Remembering the past cruel experiences,
But my smile replaces the rage as I-
Look at the falling leaves perpetuating
The future of a new beginning.
But I try not to think about it too much,
With the help of a book across the room, over a
Dust covered shelf and strawberries on the table
Saying sorry that I'm collecting new hopes.
And this is how April is becoming the month
I'd love forever.

Malleable comfort

I watch the seeds float over the thin surface
And the world cowers at its silence as it
Reaches for the bottom of its glass-made house.
And right after-
The malleable comfort
Takes place in one tiny shelter;
Soft, clumsy but shiny
And then grows into a separate direction
Sometimes early and slowly the other,
Grapples with touch and the chores of
The heightened kindness only to realize
Maybe the demure never existed
And it was a made-up fairytale.
But to remember it's fabricated light
Even in the slightest darkness, it renews
Itself into something more real and
Human, unlike me.
Finding warmth in different homes, different
Times and with better tasting wine-
Every time I dislike being too much or
Too small, too unforgettable, or too crazy-
I never had these over my plate growing up,
How did this become a way of pleasure?

Japanese saying

Flowers grew softly inside my lungs,
After every single breath that I took,
A little more than yesterday,
Because I can't pluck them out.
And I became a small part of a Japanese saying
In the words of my friend,
Because I couldn't breathe anymore from today,
Yet I still want more, I dare say.

A love letter to no-one

Heaven is in my palms
But it's hard to breathe
When you throw tantrums and I
Try to give you my forever.
I pause, wishing on the shooting star
Running my fingers through your hair
Then it seems you've fallen asleep
Like a baby who was born and then died.
I wonder if it'd be easier to not love
So much or so little at the same time.
Where do I fall on this spectrum
Of fools who rush in as soon as
They see the slightest speck of light
Headed towards nowhere.
Like a cheesy 12-year-old holding back
I look for the brightest star in the sky.
My brain observes my eyes, as they burn-
And quietly sink back into forever,
Into the bucket list of a troubled woman,
Smiling as I hear you call my name.
Spotlights? I see people running after it
All their lives. I did, too, until I didn't.
Now I'm headed towards nowhere

Sometimes resting inside your spotless-
Mind, wondering if you'll be mine
Even if forever turns out to be a lie.

Which colour would he choose

As you begin to breathe another day,
do you not finally recognize them?
The signs that are harsh and well-timed,
They know when to subtly align in my head-
When I finally believe you have changed the path
Then it turns out you're still stuck on the same page-
-just another pitfall of having an assumption.
I lie on my bed closer to sides I never chase
Turning on and off the different layers of fate.
And every week passes with another dying sky
Like another black and white cab that
Takes you from me to another smile.
I wonder if that one is better than mine
Is it warmer or cunning, and if you swing it
All over your face when you're slightly awake
Staring at the stars hanging from your grey ceiling
Making you miserable and ecstatic all at once.
And god knows how much I wish I knew everything
That is up in your mind! (I really do)
I know everything about life and death
But what's the point if it doesn't make you
Turn around and say this seems to be a better hike.

And my friends know how much I'm prepared to
Be your Stargirl and not a Sunday morning pill.
And the way you look at her was the way you looked at
me
Which makes it even harder to leave
But in all honesty, it even makes it easier to stay
Like I can finish the race and see it for myself
Who was the winner all this time- instead of
My assumptions, pierced out by the subtle signs.

Falling in love

I find happiness in different and multiple chunks
When I see you come closer and become
A more distorted version of yourself
Then all at once, I lose my train of thought
As if it didn't even exist
As if nothing else mattered
As if fairytales were true
Or it seemed like they did in those few leaps.
Standing under a thin shade of lust
Built of promises and then some more,
Which ones were true I still don't remember-
"I love you"
"I have always loved you"
"And I will forever"
Somehow they were presented in this order.
As if past ever makes sense
As if present is all you ever want
As if the future is nothing but everything that you ever asked for.
If I could ask for just one thing, what would it be?
A shade or a home I could settle in?
A sweet liar or just one truth for the rest of my life?

A freefall through silky clouds or my feet buried in the earth- forever?
I have these questions, so many of them, and I feel restless!
As if I want the answers
As if I am even ready to hear them
As if everything would turn in peace once I do.
I don’t know anything, and I don't even know if I wish to know more.

Love someone with colossal pain

You love someone utterly,
Only with a colossal pain-
You reminded me
When I liked you a little less.
I loved you for love,
And for the magic.
I loved you not with hurt,
And not for being tragic.
And when I left you
For more reliable feet,
I proudly named it me;
The arrogant me
The insatiable me
The mean me and
The broken me,
Without any fear.
And you show up now,
When pain dwells no more,
In my home?
How do I tell you,
You have nothing fruitful-
-to invest anymore?

Loving the right body

Walking to meet the one
But your intentions are named unholy,
Mildly over the boundaries,
For not loving the right body.
So you bow down a little,
Kissing the right shaped lips,
Under an unwanted rainy sky.
You have checked your apparel,
Perfect for the audience.
And in fear of not living enough,
You trade your love,
And settle for undesirable weather.
And how happy you seem
Not labelled as intrinsically unhinged.
But how unhappy you feel
Maybe you could have lived happily,
Under the wrong category,
Loving the wrong body,
Settling for perfect weather.
But fear runs through your lungs,
Like bloodshot in an insomniac,
And so you accept breathing-
-Mildly under the boundaries.

Someday

"Would you like to meet me someday"
Received and read exactly ten seconds
After they pressed send
And the plane crashed in my head again
Making unnecessary chaos awake.
I'm not brave,
When it comes to signs,
But I have met them a million times.
I have met them,
A million times
Under multiple shades
Of a pink sky.
And each time it ends up crazy
Weirdly they still like me.
And for some reason
I believe it's all fake and has no meaning.
For some reason,
I believe,
They will meet me
For the first time
Under the multiple shades
Of my blue sky-
And hope I was dead,

And wish I wasn't there,
And it was just a bad dream on a November day.

Love should be enough

"I'm not forcing you," they say
I know (catching my breath)-
I repeat for the fourth time to them,
And for the eleventh time to myself.
Lost and confused,
I try to build myself a middle ground-
I know my zodiac sign,
So I'll be convinced by the fifteenth time
I repeat myself after I lose the count.
And - love should be enough-
They would say all the time,
Wearing a faint blue jacket
Standing over the snow,
In the daytime,
In the nighttime,
In the wrong time,
In the divine time.
Love should be enough-
I undress my mind to them,
For the first time and they leave me there,
Saying I messed up.
And I'm convinced in the first time,
Because they have said that a million times before.

But I repeat to myself the words I used to fear-
Love should be enough,
As they used to say.

Goodbye

The soft wandering pink
Turns into a safe blue meadow
As the day behind sinks,
Sweetly saying goodbye.
I'll see you tomorrow-
Unless you choose not to be whole
- Both say
The light above my eyes
And the light behind, drowning in my sight.
I anticipate the last moment,
As my arms clash into its heat
And so does my beating chest,
Making the space between,
A safe place.
And I almost sense-
How synchronicity births,
Into our hearts,
And sometimes in our minds.
It gets cold,
So I let go of my force,
Let go of the intertwinement between-
My coldness and the hot breath on the other side,
Kissing me gently, the light calls it a night.

Worn out

He left the clothes given by me
Over the table, next to the leftovers.
They are twisted and layered,
Silenced and beautiful.
I used to love them,
Before he wore them.
I could wear them again
With cigarettes and silver chains.
But what if they look like-
-A body with a lost brain,
Not strong and sincerely scarred?
So I leave them where they are,
Over the table, next to the leftovers.

July Saudade

Your fingers easily swirled your brown threads,
Gracefully covering your lips, nose, eyes,
And guilt hiding some painful grits.
When we were hidden,
You would speak of love and patience.
But outside my closet,
You turned out to be mean and unpleasant.
Soyou counted till three,
One
Two
Three
And then you gifted me,
An incomplete memory,
Where my heart never wants to be touched again.

Our little piece of peace

Isn't it lovely!
How beautiful objects seem,
The shoes, the shelves, and the films we see,
when our veins feel the chill,
As their wobbly knees make a scene,
Next to the dinner table,
With a moody and dizzy greet;
Hi! Hello! Hello! Bye!
They are happy,
Knackered but proud.
But we are more,
As we cuddle in the eerie attic,
When you bring me a piece of peace,
From your small cherry lips,
Until I realize,
It's only a dream!

Letters filled with malapropisms

A love that was funny and part-time satire,
A spreadsheet of malapropisms.
They both spoke differently,
behind their wisp of curly strings.
And their hands would strike back in pockets,
when they would find themselves,
Thrown around in confusing meets.
A thousand alliterations would turn a conversation,
into a song made with love.
And the multiple attempts at knowing words that never made sense
Would feel more familiar than their tired lips.
The trials and tribulations of assassinating-
Each other's languages never found an end.
But they both found,
A long list of promises,
And admirable inhibitions.

Sanctuary of illusions

We collect chemicals in our brains,
Turn our sensible thoughts into foolish reactions,
Roll down in a room full of picture-perfect pictures,
And gather up for opportunities,
Then cry for their short-lived liveliness-
When we are left untamed in a prudent reality.
But still, fall back,
Every time you lose your chain of thoughts,
To just feel safe in a lair of failures,
To find a home in a sanctuary of illusions.

Behind the goodbye

Behind the goodbye,
From the last night,
There's a rumour spreading around,
Like bush fire.
And it's hidden from our gaze and our ears,
Yet they all know about it,
Fair enough, we say.

It dwindles in their heads,
So they stay quiet,
And make soundless noise.
We might catch a glimpse in their rooms if we try!
But do you wanna leave?
Before they start to burn us alive?
We could make a plan!
To write our story,
Before we settle in the home of stars.

Recurring landslide

I invite you to observe the fire,
A montage of desires.
I want to do so,
To present a crowd-worthy sight-
Of comfort in the late hours,
For myself, that exists just with you.
And it's true!
You'll lose your footsteps,
But I did too!
Feeling heavy with regrets,
And with lies attached to my faith.
I have had my fair share,
Of dancing inside a burning tower!
Now I'm having the time of my life,
When the landslide is revisiting,
Under the swollen feet,
But of a different liar.

Grass

Grass up to my knees,
As I walk beside a wish that was once a dream,
But now a kiss.
A wish I was born for,
Dipped in colours stolen from the home of stars,
When I saw their light, for the first time.
Now I see!
How wrong it would have been,
If a diary of a 3 feet soul,
Had chosen my journey after kindergarten growth.
A life that would have been a blessing,
But not the same as the wish that is now listening,
To me and my wordless singing.
She left the blank pages,
All these years for me,
Where now I store my footprints,
Through the medium of words that speak,
Just for my baby!
That once was a dream,
Now a gentle breeze.

The shy ghost

The shy ghost!
Shy and invisible.
Intrigued by the way,
brilliance dances over his lover's tongue.
And even most adored sonnets seem nothing,
When his lover reminisces about that one ridiculous
word.

He feels alone!
Inside his cloudy clothes,
So he eavesdrops when souls encounter pleasures.
And learns a little civility,
To impress a human he adores,
Who knows quite a few words.

He is dipped in excitement!
And drives up to the drunken hills,
To search for some new clothes,
Hoping to gaze at its lover.
They say he's just a mist!
But all he needs is to be covered in sweet grief.

Wonderwall

Dear soul friend,
Sat next to me under the chestnut trees,
Can't hear me?
But my words are deeper than you think!
Deeper than people you see,
People you observe,
And then judge them
Like the perfectionist you seem,
And a know-it-all of this dream,
You are a turtle dove for everyone's nighttime screens.

Dear soul friend,
The one I approach every night to spill some tea,
Can't see me?
But my eyes watch you for my needs,
Every second you hate,
Every minute you waste,
And every hour you stay,
In every single moment, even when it's fake,
Like a real artist, you create in this life,
And you may not know me,
But you are a Wonderwall in all my sweet dreams.

Crescent love

Dear crescent love,
Are you happy?
Now that you are not just
A burning urge anymore
But_
A word with a hundred thousand meanings
A meaningless scribble on autumn leaves
A dandelion lying quietly over words written by Anais
A black inked rose over my left wrist
And a golden chandelier in my darkened eye.
You are so much more now-
Than just a gush of infinite feelings.
Are you happy to be adored like thenew moon?

The hook

Should I say yes?
Which I have never said before!
Blame it on the travellers,
Who told me,"the street cracked right beneath our feet!"
But if I say yes,
Which I have never said before,
Will you pull my fingers with your hook,
From the hectares and hectares of deadness,
And give me time to breathe at every passing station?
So I'm still alive and pleasant?
If I say yes,
Which I have never said before,
Will all of my nightmares get abducted away?
And leave no place for my soft petals to dry and fade?
But home to bloom into new life again?

Wordsmith

I risk the consequences,
Keep the external parts of me,
Outside my window.
But the silly heart-attacks gather up,
Outside my door often.
There's mystery locked inside these walls,
Would cause injuries once out.
I light up the candles
Cinnamon and roses! Spreading throughout the room,
With butterflies flying around,
Singing the truth on drumrolls from my heart.
I write their words in my language,
On the letters sealed with your name "Mr Wordsmith"
In the ambience of a beautiful and vulnerable moment,
That I only get to share with loneliness.

King-sized

My king-sized bed!
With its shining friends;
The colossal sheets,
And fancy pillows!
Calling me into its grid.
It's a perfect night,
To settle down before 4:45.
It cares for me like nobody,
But today its oceans and oceans of softness,
Are somehow burning my skin.
It is one of those nights,
Where the stars seem shy,
Surrounded by heartbreaks and nuances,
They keep me awake.
And the red lights,
Outside this room feels like wonderful kites,
Tonight I want to catch them with both of my hands,
And then rest gracefully on my kitchen aisle.

Just friends

We have captured inside us
Our favourite past time hobbies,
Our matching t-shirts hiding symphonies,
Our obsession with bare necessities,
And the small timeframe where we don't know anything,
But only each other, intentionally.
And we know,
We are friends when we walk in together,
We are friends when we walk out together,
While keeping the 2 feet distance,
And we like being true strangers, intentionally.

Secret love

A fairy tale or a secret will!
I would never want to share it.
Who would with their snake-like grin?

A childlike grace or a perfect mess?
I couldn't fall more for it.
But I fail to paint it over my skin.

They see it like it is,
The way we want them to perceive.
And it will never get seen,
Our love will remain a secret sin.

Waiting with the birds

I see you happy,
Cheerful between the alignment of the pink and blue sea.
I watch you,
Standing on this hill, waiting for your soft sighs.
There might be a lot of space,
But here is your nest.
Not yours to save one,
But I know how not to memorize some stuff!
So there will always be a seat,
Safer than those black and white streets,
Because some flowers always wait for unlikely things.

Daydream

It would be great if I could pastiche everything,
From the night we met!
From head to toe,
Start to end,
And from the little,
To the bigger awakenings
It would be nice to have that;
A coven of lost memories!
But it is quite hard to search for them,
In this reality.
Yet I see that night,
Every time I reach for the darkness,
Sleeping underneath my eyes.

The one

The tiny pit on your right cheek
Itburns a hole inside so deep,
And your brown glass made stones
Paint rainbow storms in my brain.
And you should know,
I hate you sometimes!
Because I have lost some things since you arrived,
Things I will never understand.
You must live a hundred more years as per my mother's unusual jokes!
Cause you show up everywhere, every time I think of you.
She says I have gained some mood swings,
And I blame it on your invisible visits.
You must be a magician!
The one they used to talk about in my dreams,
When I was only three feet!
Cause you make me smile,
Even when you stand on different land.
You are not in my world yet,
But I believe you will end up being the one.

False love

I was a happy child,
The favourite one, all my life.
Then this life came along,
Where I saw him and it was sincerely insane.
And the way his words carved him in my head
Turning him into a rose gold lake.
It gave me a chance
To feel something, something different
Maybe to become lethal.
And so I became a fresh bite of regrets
In the early mornings-
An intangible feed for his sour tongue.
And for my eyes to live in rage and to live with lonely gaze,
"So mote it be," he says.

Lover

They wrote in the newspaper,
This is the end!
This is the start!
This is the first time!
This is the last time!
Everything is here!
Everything is gone!
But then a sound of a soul,
Settles down everything,
And gives hope in a home,
Where the fears refuse to run away!
It is a sound of a soul, but the voice of a lover
And now it's quiet again.

I could

Believed I could never jump for someone,
with an escaping disposition!
But I fell hard,
At the bottom of salt filled land,
And had my wings tear into scrapes,
Like my mother's faith.

Thought I could get back on my feet,
Like a phoenix from a grim!
But there's no atmosphere,
To catch my breath,
There's nothing but a thousand fears.

Eighth grade (last memory)

Parked my feet outside a building
Familiar than most faces I met yesterday
And I stood there wondering,
Like a spire on the top of a building near the beach.
Sparked my eyes, as if they saw the sky for the first time
After quite a second, I realized-
-it was a place where I used to be invisible.
Back in eighth grade
Back was the blue, red, and black watch on my left wrist
And back was a contagious smile,
Continued with a hand curved around my waist
And as it grew further-
-its sleeves shrivelled up like a scared bird in its nest
But back were not the faces always being incensed by my steps.
A song played from behind like a radio underwater,
We were mimicking a silent film.
Scarred my mind halfway through the campus
When the machine counting my last tears
Decided to give me no attention
And its last beep vanished with my last memory of forever.

Difference between then and now

Back then, turning a distressed smile
Into an urge of running through a marigold field
Now calling it a distraction blamed on my name

Back then, a scenario to be belonged in
And asking more of it till it slips deep in grief
Now is a past that was wasteful in every possible way

Back then, a short and sweet melody
Many said clingy but you called it worthwhile
Now it's a running joke even in your mind

Back then, it had every reason to fly
And together was celebrated as forever
Now it has no right to intervene even in your dreams

Back then, it ran further close to the silver line
Turning the twisted road a little divine
Now it's being stuck in someone's disappearance

Back then,
Even nothing was everything

Even broken danced endlessly
Even hurtful felt timidly growing, now
It's just a smug left on a familiar face
And shame ready for revenge.

2 am loner

I was daydreaming again, unlike my sibling
In the mucky and sweet air stuck between
The four blue walls. Just enough blue to
Narrow down someone's attention to every
Object in the room but the walls.
And there was a great sense of humour
Swallowing everyone who stood there,
Besides the two of us in the corner
(you and me) and I made sure I was more
Cornered to feel safe and not have a single
Thread of scandal wrapped around me.
(you were bright as the sun and I was as
Insignificant as a broken piece of the moon)
Could never belong in the same world
But there we were, close and human.
I was happy to be there and,
Sad because I knew it wouldn't last long.
Then happier again, I could always
Come back again to live again.
But I stopped right away. I made a mistake.
I didn't picture it the way I wanted to feel.
It was beautiful but less elegant, and I'm as
Concerned about my visions as a loner is

About solitude and resurrection.
I stopped right away, plucking the thorns out
Of the thin air and I knew I couldn't go back
To that pursuit because I was left as colourless
As the water and as blue as the four walls
Of that room. Never built to love or carry
Soft admiration.

She knows

I am just a little child to her
And like a daughter, I tell her everything
Except I keep everything in my diary to scream.
She doesn't know I didn't get rid of all the songs last night
Until I got discarded by the morning light.
She doesn't know I tried too hard but failed to find something
That could get at least the colour of my eyes right.
She doesn't know that I tried to uncover someone's pile of secrets
But forgot to hide the hurricane packed up in my mind.
But she knows there will be another night and morning light
And I won't be replaced by a better song recommendation.
And she knows that I learned early on that it would be less
Painful if I let the pain be mine for a while.
And I know I will eventually stop falling for someone's devious smiles.

Threatening and scandalous

When you shoved yourself_
_Into my childhood bravery,
I didn't know,
You were bad,
And for that I was senseless.

Everything that has ever met me,
And my weak screams,
Has gone down crashing,
For being its origin.

And I hate to be_
_The one who speaks in greed,
But I hope you get
This closure,
Again and again,
Till your dying day.

I don't remember your imagery,
That too has crashed down under a_
_Fearful feeling
But I still recall the sound,
Reaching to me,

As threatening and scandalous.

Though the life of your memory,
Has expired long ago,
Like an unwanted coke_
_Left alone in a vintage store
I still live in it,
Briefly and vicariously
Through a kindred spirit
As it roars at the top of its lungs,
And goes back to cry in the basement.

Wedding bells

A bride's bangles become her wedding bells
I realize it was the same for my mother
The bangles round and red-
-sound like a rumble in a prison cell.

I am told that I could take care of it
If I let myself be not known as busy
Or they could cut the strings
Taking care of the grief
If they know better.

Into a thin paper met with unavoidable ink
Suddenly the prison doesn't exist
Wait- it's still in my head
At least it's there, safe.

And I have found a man
In a place clustered with dreamy light
He seems marvellous and I could
Spend a million hours in his impeccable eyes.

But I am my mother's daughter, just like her
I have my wrists built just like her, maybe smaller-

-thrilled at the thought of the wedding aisle
And partly lost, fishing for a prison cell.

The carpenter

Dear carpenter,
Thank you!
I hate it here.
And every passing year,
Your dirty work haunts
Even more in this home.

Pathetic screams the walls_
_For hiding their true ugly colours,
Since day one from the visitors.
And the furniture never allows me to rest,
And I say it's unfair,
Cause I don't like them either!
Let alone breathe in its long-winded
Suffocation,
Sprinkled all over my chest.

I'm disgusted for so many years,
But no one comes to confirm your dirty work,
But how will they if they are not invited?
And how should I call them_
_if I am locked inside?
Dear carpenter,

Thank you very much!
Maybe I'll never like it here.

Towering enemies

I calculated the drop_
from top to bottom!
All the stars were towering like kings,
Watching me fall, they felt more like enemies.
And in the dullness of the grief,
When my breath was getting lonely,
I found my final need.
I was only a few months away,
From breaking the cage,
Still naive!
Wondered how I could hurt them.
I did break them as a victory on my dying day!
But I failed, and so did my royal friends.

The marionette doll

A little marionette doll
A mad girl
A fumbling poet
Circling round and round
In search of some lively ghosts

A world of tales
A pair of eyes
A little heart
She'd roleplay
The good old girl with grace
Perhaps, they might like a pretty face

A sensual party
A billion people
A smile that forgets the truth
Clones are hidden everywhere
And they enjoy melting all over your flesh

We die every day

We die on our death day
And sometimes days before
-crying on the bathroom floor,
Under a casual fear.
A comical casual for the villain
And a threatening one for another.
Casual like suffocating someone to death
Until they ask for another breath.
Casual like baking someone a cake
Served with a glorifying grudge against them.
Casual like hunting someone
Under a cackle of unhealthy crave.
Casual, until they aren't scared enough
To speak their brave words
Held in for days.
We die on our death day,
But sometimes days before,
Under a casual fear.

My ocean cave

I have been here many times before
The first time was
When I couldn't find the road.
I come here very often
When I cry
When I smile
When I scream
And as I spread my stack of emotions on the cold white stones
The waves hug me around my soul
And the rocks sing me tales about myself that I don't know.
But every time I come here, they come for me as well,
In their ships, chanting my name in the air.
They think I'm lost
Or perhaps I'm alone.
But I'm not.
They try to seduce me with their pearls and rain collected from heaven!
And I know if I licked them, it would taste like royalty and freedom.
But they'd pollute my lair
Feeding into my lust and fears.

And I will eventually go back to them
But for now
I'll stay here
In my little ocean cave.

Never thinks twice

I never think twice,
When I see one thing shine.
And I ignore all the thousand rings,
Just to make me free.
I step over things,
As they try to crush my feet.
Sleep next to them,
As they dwindle my dreams into haunting screams.
They seem nice!
But are they a good sign?
They give me comfort, but they lead me
into a home filled with unwanted riots.
And when my limbs are freezing outside,
They seclude me inside a suffocating mind.
I know I don't think twice,
But are they still not a good sign?

Perfection

In the past,
In the future and,
In the present,
I want to play life like a harp.
I crave the stars!
Like the beauty of the innate scars.
The flaming nerves that could cause,
A million sunrises formy eyes,
And enough urges,
To make my head touch infinite skies.
And if the internal existence is put on fire,
The blaze would seem perfect for my desires.

The mediocre genius

I close my eyes,
Watch the green and blue neon lines dancing around,
As I delve into the black hole beneath them.
I dive deeper,
To find ideas about intellectualism,
Think of places,
Where I can call myself a genius!
As somebody, someone can rely on,
The one the mind is hungry for.
I cling to many layers of my little naivety,
And pray to find at least one string clean,
That I can hold on to finally.
I let myself get tangled in the pitch-black sheet of
foolishness,
But I am still not a genius yet!

Seed

Something that was meant to bloom
Is distilled into a thread of guilt
Which should have been
A permanent charisma to oneself
Now keeps urging to be liked by everyone else.
I was born to become the universe of my desire,
How come I beg for applause_
from a crowd of hundreds of liars.

Searching myself in the quiet melodies

I search for myself in places,
Where it's just me, but no rush.
And try to quieten the world outside my flesh,
The yells, the rumours, the mumbled melodies,
The best nights, the unlearned lessons,
And the neglected screams,
Where it's just me.
I try to collect a brief moment,
Where every inch of my body is numb for a quite second,
And the world outside stays outside,
Like teenage rage unbothered by the substances in their brains.
I stroll inside my mind like a walk in a busy bar,
And I try to search for the quiet corners,
That is quite alive.
The quiet and the disconnected version of my film,
Where for once, the characters are not empathizing with every single face,
Where every scene is thrilling,
But everyone's favourite villain falls apart.

Standing in a bog

Feels like standing in a golden bog of lies,
In the middle of a thunderstorm.
People warning around,
Screaming, "you are tragic!"
And so I agree, "I am strong too!"
But if it was true,
There would be no excuses,
No yells,
No warnings,
No questions,
No answers,
And no fistfights.

Moment of curse

The moment that feels like a vial of the curse!
Fingers dwindling and fidgeting,
Water drops swirling around dusty cheeks,
And breathing takes a brief ride of guilt.

And when I see the clock,
It is past the finish line.
Yet it is still here,
Which is making me unaware of myself.

My bright eyes stuck,
In the state of wavering faith.
It stays around like wild breezes,
Over the tombstones,
Like an unwanted best friend.

Gregarious people

Gregarious people,
Who live in flocks,
Who never say goodbye,
I admire them,
I ache to be them.
The people, the lights, the smoke, and their muses,
And the ruby of someone's eyes,
I want to be that too!
But I'm not sure,
If I will be able to intertwine myself with them?
Will I ever understand these conversations and connections,
That has become a definition of good existence?
Will I ever be able to indulge more than a lonely goodbye,
And a half cheerful hello?
Will I ever be on their team?
Or will I always be a passing kid,
Intrigued by their fashion skills?

Unfamiliars

I'm at a thousand miles distance,
Yet I hear the sound of the ocean.
The sweet crackling walks of the waves,
I don't hear anything else.

I have never been to a circus,
Yet I see them; the freaks!
The unfamiliars of this bubble consider me one of them,
I don't see anything else.

Where am I?
Who am I?
Am I one of them?
Am I anything to them?
I can hear nothing but them,
I'm everywhere but here.

The carnival

The carnival goes around,
All night, all day, all summer and winter.
Some eyes do visit!
A formality they do, for a good friend,
I'm to them.
And some don't even bother,
I'm none of their problems.
Then there are strangers,
Watching from the sidelines,
Still unbothered, just passing their time,
Until their cars arrive.
I stay here,
Listening carefully to every echo,
Made by every scary ride and every death it brings to my eyes.
I sit here,
In the dust and the deranged notions
left behind by people I don't remember.
Cautiously trying to make sense of it,
Slowly trying to scrape each of them,
Only to be left dazed by their unfriendliness.

My perfect tear

I cry,
In these faithless seconds
Was it a bad day,
Was it a bad deed,
Was it bad greed,
when a tear drops from my left eye?
It keeps dropping,
I keep stroking it away,
Leaving my right eye dry and alone.
Now all I want is
To have a happy dream,
All I want is,
To cross this line,
Into a happy scene.
So I can weep a happy tear,
Next to my right ear,
Which will make a perfect tear!

After this?

So where are we left after this?
Somewhere between the destabilized homes and,
the green path leading to a new land of a new beginning?

Some part of us wants to stay,
But all of me wants to take the chance!
To see if there's a fate,
That would make more sense.

People are what I am a small part of,
But I linger in the world where they don't belong,
So far.

No wonder!
They don't like something that is just me instead of a gift,
And I have sorrows swinging around like sirens,
Around the walls, they kept me in.

Slower days

I live on slower days!
Half of me is half awake and aware that I'm running,
From the storm, the chaotic waves, and the messy creatures.
The other half of me,
Does not remember anything,
And everything seems to put me off.

I live on slower days!
Secure from the tears, the emotions, and the precarious vulnerability.
It's better this way,
Being unbothered by anything,
And every mistake seems to be a muddled memory.

Tick tock

Tick tock tick tock!
The fingers striking down from the clouds,
Into the blue waters.
Drowning or dancing?
Both have the same meaning for them now.
And the screaming of the heart,
Excites the cells to rush faster,
Making it believe,
There is something more to this billowy,
Than the rumoured nightmares and deaths,
More than the stories spread by the legends of this great vastrealm,
To quell the attraction it holds,
So no one can trail behind its gold,
And its hidden mysteries.

A quick roll

Where to next?
A quick roll from above,
The whole world turned around,
I can't see,
And I can't hear anymore.
Everything has distorted,
From happiness to sadness,
Now that my feet are beneath this ground.

Accidents

Accidents kept happening,
And everyone denied it.
Our sky was falling,
While the rooms were burning red,
And hearts in darkest blue.
Things happened but made sense,
As everyone sang one last time,
With mourn in their eyes.
We all were here,
We all knew some fallen trees wouldeventually crush our skin,
Someday, somewhere.
But we simply forgot to wear our helmets,
As we dressed up for our march,
In our cars to catch some scars.

Plenty of night

Plenty of night is still here!
I hear the stillness my heart wielded,
With screams from the nearby rooms,
And smell the sickness of the almost dead.
The anticipation for this night to end,
Keeps swinging back and forth in my chest.
The desperation to see the first light,
Without burning these hours for too long,
Keeps getting bigger and bigger.
But I'm still here,
In this endless night.

Lighted candle

A lighted candle!
Once was a picture of comfort,
Now a wisp of smoke.
And how parallel the end seems_
With her and with you
With him and with me.
In the presence of nothing and everything,
Fading away through the ordinary gates,
To somewhere we don't know yet,
To travel in the ambience of invisible grains.

My feathers

I standstill,
But out of place are my feathers!
Makes me feel fragile,
And like the cursed night.

The road ahead is misty,
Am I a flying creature?
Or am I supposed to haunt this road,
Just to be buried later in the same place?

Should I stay here in peace,
Until someone finds me?
Or am I supposed to befriend these never-seen beings,
As I walk down the road ahead with them?

Maybe don't

A blackout in a white dress

In the moment of grace

The river is stuck again with glowing stars

But only I know they are a million scars.

Frosty and pale goes my face

Quickly in front of all of my friends,

Caught up in fragments of comatose.

I'm afraid!

Don't want to interrupt them,

But I do need some help.

And then I hear in soft whispers

Succumbed to hellish fears

"Maybe don't", so I won't!

But do get me some help

If you see me struggling

In the moment of grace.

Bad architecture

Ruins of this house
Seem so beautiful
But are writing down my past, my present, my future
With words, I will never desire.
"Wicked and unworthy",
The cracked walls want to write me off so casually.
All of them are building up multiple stories
With broken windows for a widow
And with a darkened floor for a sightless soul.
They are doing it willingly
While their hearts are getting stoned
_ and burned down in the backyard.

Some day they might understand

My fingers feel the change in the wind
Realize how the ground under my feet is freezing.
I am standing quietly on one side of the street,
On the other side, my friends wave me goodbye!
And someday they might understand,
I wasn't late on purpose,
I am not burning the hours alone,
I am not enamoured with ghosting,
And I am not just another fable in their lives,
I am here to stay for them and their dreams,
Hoping they won't push me out,
Like they did my dreams.

A love affair with the shades of dependency

Too proud to notice!
Too deeply in love with accompanied loneliness!
But I still kiss my thanks to god,
Cause I got lucky enough,
To grow as the moss over the green and blue walls,
Finally, being granted to breathe.
So I don't look up that the sky has struck_
Me with the absence of rain,
And down where the pond snail is eating up my cells.
Too old to be curious,
And too distracted to realize,
There should be a piece on a different side,
Made for just me and my soul.
Where they cry for me,
Every night like a newborn child,
While I am stuck in these upside-down lights.
I am just too in love with these shades of dependency
That is dressed up as love poetry.

Parent trap

I still try to know you
Through old pictures and
Decades-old conversations.
It's a dream
That remains_
Unchecked onmy bucket list.
A challenge
Where I try to give my everything
Never mind the hurdles
And never talk about the bridges
That don't bring us closer,
But strike back at me like
Snakes when I climb the ladder
And quietly faint,
Every single day.
So I put a trap
Hoping I won't fail
And you'll learn
You are meant to stay
And not to run away.

The lady of visions

The lady of visions,
Who lived only in her room!
The orchids who loved her,
Say she was forever a lover.

Tied with the traditions of a predecessor,
Was obliged to leave behind her clothes under the furniture,
She absorbed the false! Thinking she might receive some love.

The time she spent in her room,
Was all the time she ever knew.
Talking to orchids dancing in the water,
Weaving visions out of her fascinations,
That remained nowhere but in the dreams she slaughtered.

While she died unknown,
But to her beloved orchids,
She was forever known,
The one who was a lover.

The one who was once kind

Belittling the wheel of fortune,
Prodigal with little to no empathy.
Once was so kind,
Now known as the last one to kiss the sky!

Slowly is burning,
At the stake of the lost meaning of love.
Will never be considered again,
Will never be rescued from his tangled fate.

The birds and the people

The birds had more to say,
Than the couples seated at the bar.

Both content with happiness,
But one of them was half not!

Both deemed the beauty the sky held,
Capturing in their lenses,
But one of them saw the big picture,
While the other rooted for the hidden stars.

Both wanted to frolic in the gentle air,
Realizing nothing could ever stop them,
But one of them was brutally caged.

Offspring of the passed ones

Offspring of the passed ones,
Taken care of by the new loved ones.
Sowing seeds of love and dreams,
Mistaken for wrong deeds.
Who is true? Who is not?
Nobody wants to ever find out.
They keep hiding away,
The tears emanated from the dreary care
So no one catches a glimpse of hatred,
So they keep the troubled hearts,
Rue the forced bonds,
And so the story goes on.

The Water

The water gulped the dust down!
The greyer and the older ones first.
Men with the most brutal and unearthly growls,
Some were dead,
Some were still breathing,
Flowing through the long body,
Like the royalty in their blood,
And slavery in their palms.
All together in the same boat,
Reverting towards their home.

Lover with memories

Ruined the memories,
Mocked the beautiful sceneries,
Little by little,
They were collected by an innocent,
Who sought nothing but love,
Like the only drug one could ever trust,
Like a place that could always be found as home.
Now, all that he sees is the dead-end of the street,
Built for the lovers from Greece,
As a mockery of their beliefs.

Replete with hunger

Replete with a hunger to avenge,
That is nothing but revenge.
Soft yet sharp are her canine teeth,
The eyes revolve around every stare,
For every length of blood, it could taste.
Cautiously taking every step,
Optimistic about the journey with an iota of alarm,
The lady of the jungle, fearful to none,
Arrives to feed her cubs.

The fruitless heart

The heart once considered fruitless,
Will eventually go on to translate the language of love,
Through his variegated words.
The one that always got mushed,
When found in the perishable social contracts of this world,
Will be known as the poet in every decade,
For a hundred more years.
The murmur of his dysfunctionality,
Itwill turn into an appreciation,
And a billboard shining beneath the confetti.
A boy who was just a regular,
With glasses over his crooked nose,
Will own every single part of this world.

Subtle mysteries

Subtle mysteries reflecting in her eyes!
Subtle, deep, brown, and alien.
Harmonizing with the satin over her skin,
The emerald green is so rich.
The luxury dancing throughout her body,
Every edge and every peck that exists,
Covering and detaining all of her sorrows.
How do you word her existence though?
Maybe just some broken pieces of glass,
Disparaged itself in the desperation to be kissed,
By everyone she knows and by everyone who knows her.

The soldier in the mirror

In the mirror he sees,
Himself and no one else,
With the curled down hair that lengths above his soft ruffle,
Dipped in the blood of many that were never innocent,
Matching the dignity in his heart,
Are his angelic eyes; proud.
How little he felt before
Laughs now knowing,
He never was so brave when controlled.

Her midsummer love

She missed the midsummer touch,
And the stranger who was,
Just a temporary lover.
She missed everything that was no more here,
And how they gave themselves fake names,
Just to haste the first phase.
She missed everything,
The mornings and the shores,
And how its ending was sweet and sour.

There once was a girl

There once was a little girl,
And she used to be very happy,
And she would love to share her love,
For love with everyone around her.
But then she was sad; how miserable she felt!
Growing in the search for treasure to fill up space inside her lungs.
So she found a way to eat and to eat and then eat some more,
She felt happier again! Never like before!
Until she realized she was all alone,
She had eaten some of her friends.
So then she starved and starved and then starved some more,
But never felt happy,
Ever again.

A night in a motel

A night in a motel,
With friends and ignorants.
Surrounded by addictions and sorrows,
Where she saw him!
Lighting up the stars; the bearer of the deranged ones,
Seemingly unassuming at first sight,
But an ocean filled with golden skies.
She prayed that this mortal would stay,
And this fate -
Would bring a lot of hope for her to stay.

Sleepwalkers

There was a world of sleepwalkers.
A world dressed up in muddy grey suits and corsets,
Carrying their wealth over their shoulders.
A world made of concrete and papers dipped in
manipulative ink.
They used to scream at the top of their metal lungs
"We did it!"
Thinking they got the approval from above and outside
their world.
And they still live somewhere,
Drinking the tears they shed when no one came.

The voracious

Lurking in the eclipse
Scary and beautiful
Warm and creepy
They hunt the lone wolf.
They gift him a kind hug,
And an amiable place to live free.
Ravenous stares but their laughs are balmy,
They let him stay, they let him sleep and they let him breathe_
And cautiously learn him.
Strong but naive and unaware,
Falling in love with each of these pleasures,
Adores his brand new friends.
They are not good nor bad,
But he sure is nothing like them,
And falls into their rabbit hole.
Boldly takes a new shape that is none,
Not them and not itself
But just a hunted slave.
Just an ugly shape left to be burnt,
With one last moment of pride,
To see the end so near and so cruel.
And when he smiles one last time,

It hits like a bullet to many of its kind.
Like an omen,
Like a warning sign,
Like the last cloud in the sky,
Puts them at the edge of an awful time.
Who will proceed with good fate?
The observers and the passersby watch,
As they rewind the good old tales,
The future quivers inside their head;
_Escaping to a far off land
Where no eyes can cry,
No light can shine,
And no echo can rise.
There's no black and white,
No sun or its rise,
It's just him
And his fearful cries.

The dualist

She is a dualist!
A soldier on the daytime,
Making friends even on the enemies land,
Harbouring emotions of peace,
Then goes back to becoming a part of the sin,
In the nighttime.
And sometimes she is the sin itself,
Which shows through her arms and above her knees.
But you won't see it,
Since she is covered in clothes and inks.
They show through like planes wandering too far,
In the plain skies that is her skin.
She is coloured in awful red,
That would make you run away,
But you won't see it,
Since she is hidden behind a mouth,
That fakes a beautiful smile.

The girl on her way

Little girl on her way,
Enlightening some brains,
And collecting little stars,
For her jar.
Ferocious are her dreams,
Heightened by the way she sees,
Everything.
Naive a little,
A little brave;
On a path no one else would ever take.

Ink spilled all over the leaves

Words they wrote-
-And then rewrote,
Till they found their meaningful place,
Now I write them-
-And rewrite them,
Until they rhyme and they are completely mine,
Hoping they'll find a meaningful fate.
They are authentic,
Travelling the desired reality,
With a big chunk of uncertainty.
We take what we love,
And leave the rest in cold and dust.
They are the turning off of dull lights,
When things don't look right,
And our minds are too tired of logical fights.
They are what we see,
Set of perfect daydreams,
Universally clean,
The ink spilled all over the leaves.

Camera roll purge

I explore things into my camera roll purge,
Thanking the volunteers who showed up every time,
Starting from the laugh over a fall during lunch.

I stumble upon a smile caught in the mid of a crime,
It's me provoked in an unwashed pyjama,
Sneaking out and tiptoeing on a summertime night.

In my head, I turn on the music made by Lana,
As I come across a lady showcasing flower power,
In her early years, she was enamoured by Madonna.

Then I see a tall human known as the spitfire,
My father seems frustrated at the television drama,
And my sister is wearing a floral frock in the corner.

I almost cry at a picture of a kid watching Dora,
He once, at age eight, gave me thecold shoulder,
Now I revengefully rely on karma.

In the end, I watch myself becoming older,
And I smile at the camera holding a grudge.

Magpie

Oh, magpie!
From countrysides to city lakes,
Flying into the garden,
I wish you were flying in my garden,
As if a gift flying into my arms;
Silver as jewellery found in a jewellery box,
Golden like the heavy work carved on its lead,
Dusty, as if it was hidden like a treasure under the bed,
Shining like a star that never crumbled into fragments,
Lovable like a writer's admiration for his oeuvre of years.

Oh, magpie!
From countrysides to city lakes,
Flying into a garden,
I wish you never fly into the one I water,
As if a car crashing into my bones;
Unknown like a foreign country not making sense,
Obsessive like limerence evolving through every kiss,
Blue like a lark singing on blue early morning,
Distant like a vague dream you don't think you'll ever see again,
Twisted like a hanging rope figuring its way around a neck.

Who am I?

Who am I?
A tinyfreckle of mortality,
Or a speckle of every being I have ever seen?
A city stalker or a nighttime author?
I have sung my tale exactly how I know it to be,
Yet my words don't sound meant to be.
Am I a caged bird,
living inside a mirage?
And sometimes screens that I never clean?
I'm not a liar!
But what if,
Everything I have ever felt,
Is just a long sleep of desired dreams?
Who am I?
And will I ever be free?

Winter

I like summer but also-
-Warmly crying in my sweater
My sister puts the blankets away
I can't deny her acknowledging the best
She knows winter is floating away
But I dislike how quickly it's happening
And I dislike she's the one to take note of it
Even though I'm supposed to be aware of it first
Since I love the trees dancing under the wavy heat
And yellow lolly over my tongue turning me cool and sweet
Since I love getting lost in the car when it's hot
And yellow sundress over my skin making me pretty
But no one needs to know-
I'm very much in love with winter for now
Which is floating away and realigning with a goodbye.

In the wind

Find me in the wind!
When the sun rises, softly touching your skin,
That is slightly filled with cuts and bruises from your grief,
Found in the pit of a juvenile dream.

Find me in the wind!
When the mystical beings of October,
Finally, start to weave from their manifested fields,
In the burning hours of a clementine evening.

Find me in the wind!
When the lost hues of love,
Have finally found their way back home,
To get lost in the early summer morning kissing.

And find me in the wind!
When the gifts of autumn start to fade again,
As winter will welcome itself,
With its most awaited wonders.

Blueprint of this journey!

Eyes are the blueprints of our journey,
From this world to the other side!
A simple but fragile instrument that will play along,
Till we reach the end of this river.
It will carry the notes and letters of some unrequited love,
And some theories of some unrelenting emotions,
Encapsulated inside the tears.
“Be careful, be cautious!” they always say,
As much as they are faithful,
They will never be found again,
Once lost inside this world.

Hailstones

Hailstones never knock on our doors,
Before hitting the earth,
Just for the sake of soothing the unsettling souls.
They just fall,
Fall,
And fall!
While you do nothing at all,
But watch it create a whole storm,
Neighbouring our warm souls.
Its light existence,
Is breathtakingly beautiful,
But tragically destructive,
To all the green and yellow pieces,
Of the trees that live in your backyard.
Hailstones are pretty!
But they never knock before their arrival.

Death

How powerful is death!
Known as the most awaited guest,
Yet the most brutal friend.

Makes sense to someone who suffered colossal pain,
But is just another undesirable flaw,
To someone who's fallen in love.

The power of death is so unbearably fascinating,
When it stands weak in front of none.
It lives nowhere,
But it is found in every edge through every lens!

Pine trees

Cold mountain trees,
They call them pine so serene!
I'm diving into the brave air with my cracked heels
With a lover I met, he's a little bit of a meek
Barging through the silent cries of fortunate endings
I know, quite typical of me.

Now everything makes sense!
Why loving is easy-
When we give our first cry and gift our last smiles,
When we come as dust, introduce our blood,
And then again leave as dust_
For forever.

Town

Standing on top of the tallest cliff!
In the smallest town,
Of this big world.
And I can see people like stars,
While they fathom something I can't.

I see colours in your eyes,
As you see colours in the sky between your_
Peace out signs you're throwing in my way.
I see you watch time,
As it takes you to another_
Paradise.

And then slowly,
You take three inches off of your feet.
Giggling in the streams,
When your toes get tickled by the pebbles,
As you walk into another_
Autumn sky.

Change

I see butterflies,
Around every corner and,
Every turn,
The omen of change itself.
I see them every second of my life,
Sincerely trudging around me,
Pointing out the similarities between both of us.
Does my life bring changes too?
Being the outcomes of my judgments?

Blue and yellow

Blue and yellow,
How do you go along so well, no matter where you stand?
Overlapping between the horizons and the ground,
And dancing in my school's drawing palette.
Do you weep when one of you outshines the other?
Or do you make compromises knowing,
The end is near?
Do you hate it when you realize,
You are not alike?
Or do you celebrate with each other?
Do you end yourself for the sake of your ego?
Or do you always hold each other to make the grass greener?
Dear blue and yellow,
Is there a lot that I need to learn through your sight?

The first thing

The first thing noticed about the flower_
She breathes in the wind that came from wherever her beloved has touched the ground,
Lost in the longing to meet him before he leaves for another world.
And it's beloved_
He sips the nectar,
To let her know he's finally here for her.
How precious is this act of love!
But how long will it be till he finds himself,
A new lover?
To leave her behind with a forever she believes in,
As she suffers?

My bluebird

My bluebird!
The days are numbered,
But how lovely day it is to see your whole,
How grateful to know I'm still not alone.
You will be though,
And so will I.

But till we are not,
We let the sun smile on our faces together,
We see the same stars,
Each time, each of them with love,
And amazement.

And in solitude,
Wherever we go,
I shall end this pursuit,
At the same breath,
As you! my love.

That early autumn morning!

That early autumn morning
I met a firefly near the lake
Fell in love with his greets
And then followed him into his crib.

That early autumn morning
When the leaves looked more like pages
So I wrote him a letter of love
As he loved me without any care.

That early autumn morning
He didn't leave for his homeland
I said it would lead to a dreadful fate
But for him, it was still not December yet

That early blue morning
I cried with a roaring pain
My love was dead in the frozen lake
Cause December was finally here.

Here

We are five in total,
Fine with one being closed off.
Three of us pose like our hero jack,
Feeling like a little shy,
Flying high in the colourful sky.
We are now four in total,
Fine with one gone too far.

We are young and in motion,
Drunk searching for the oceans.
Aggressive but naive dreamers,
Dancing on our own,
Yet getting ready for the one.
We are a little older now,
But wilder than the giant stars.

We are far off from the oceans,
Isolated from the motions.
Impressive with the almost truth of life,
Hiking up several minds,
And exploring every single height.
We are still here,
But confined by growing scars.